HOW TO TRAIN
A DOG

A Step-by-Step Approach to Canine Obidience and Behavior.

Timothy G. Williams

TABLE OF CONTENTS

OVERVIEW

Dog training is essential for a harmonious pet-owner relationship. It creates a clear channel of communication so that your dog is aware of expectations. A well-trained pet avoids behavioral problems and becomes a well-adjusted member of your family and the community. It also guarantees their security by immediately complying with directions. Furthermore, learning and mental stimulation are essential to their wellbeing. Establishing trust through training strengthens the link between you and your animal friend.

The foundation of a healthy connection with your dog is affection, respect, and trust. Play and work out together while spending valuable time. Their faith in you as their leader is strengthened by your steady, kind leadership. Reward good behavior and give compliments to strengthen the relationship. Recognize their needs and indications to promote mutual understanding. Empathy and patience foster a loving atmosphere that deepens your bond with your faithful friend.

CHAPTER ONE

Getting Ready For Training

Choosing the Best Training Techniques for the Breed and Personality of Your Dog

It's critical to adjust training techniques to your dog's breed and attitude. To comprehend a breed's innate inclinations, research its traits. For example, retrievers like interactive play, but herding dogs can benefit from more regimented regimens. Take into account your dog's disposition; some dogs respond well to praise, while others might need more forceful direction. Modifying techniques guarantees efficient, customized training for a contented, well-mannered pet.

Compiling Necessary Training Materials

Acquiring necessary training materials is the first step toward successful dog training. Start with a strong collar and leash to provide a safe and secure walking relationship. Differently valued treats are used as rewards for good behavior. Interactive puzzles and chew toys are good sources of brain stimulation. A cozy bed and crate provide a secure retreat for sleeping and potty training. Reinforcement is aided by training tools like as whistles and clickers. Cleaning and comfort are guaranteed by grooming tools. In addition, think about housebreaking training pads or mats. To provide a favorable environment for productive and pleasurable training sessions, make an investment in high-quality supplies that are customized to your dog's size and demands.

Creating a Regular Training Program

In dog training, having a regular training program is essential. Routine establishes predictability, which aids in your dog's comprehension of expectations. Allocate a specific period of time every day for brief and targeted training sessions. Start with simple commands and add new abilities one at a time. To help in learning, pick a place that is calm and free of distractions. Choose periods when your dog is alert and responsive by keeping an eye on their energy levels. Maintaining consistency helps your dog learn and keep orders more easily. This schedule helps to create a feeling of consistency and order in the pet, making them more obedient and well-adjusted to different circumstances.

CHAPTER TWO

Basic Obedience Training

Sit: Your dog will be encouraged to sit on command with this basic command. Hold the treat first near their nose and then gradually lift it above their head.

Their bottom will naturally drop as their head chases the treat. As soon as they sit, tell them to "Sit" and give them a reward. To reinforce this instruction, consistency and repetition are essential.

Stay: It's critical to teach "Stay" for safety. Your dog should start off sitting. Say "Stay," extend your palm, and step backward. Give them kudos and a treat if they remain still. Increase the duration and distance gradually. To ensure dependability, practice this command in a variety of situations.

Lie Down: This instruction promotes composure. Your dog should begin by sitting down. Treats should be held to the nose and then lowered to the floor. Say "Lie Down" and give them a reward as they follow. Continue, then progressively cut back on the treat. Practice in various settings to make the command more solid.

 This command guarantees prompt recall, which is essential for security. Start at a safe location. Hunch down, extend your arms, and call out to them, "Come." Give them your full encouragement. When they get to you, give them praise and rewards. Increase the distance gradually. Continuity strengthens a trustworthy memory.

"Leave It": This command keeps your dog from snatching or eating anything dangerous. Take an inexpensive thing in your hand to begin. Once they become disinterested, give them a different goodie and close your hand and say, "Leave It." Practice resisting more and more temptations.

Heel: It's good for walk s whe n your dog can walk

quietly by your side. Start by putting them on a leash. Put a goodie down by your side and get moving. When they stay close, say "Heel" and give them something. To help this behavior stick, practice it frequently and give it praise.

Applying Strategies of Positive Reinforcement

When training dogs, positive reinforcement is a very effective method. In order to promote the repeat of desired behaviors, it entails rewarding them. Give your dog lots of praise and food, cuddles, or toys whenever they follow instructions or behave well. They associate this favorably, which makes them more willing to comply going forward. Rewarding favorable behavior promptly and consistently is essential. Reward-based strategies should be avoided since they may instill confusion or anxiety. Your dog will become well-adjusted and ready to please as a result of positive reinforcement, which also deepens the link between you and your dog. It produces a pet that is content, self-assured, and receptive, which makes training enjoyable for you both.

Effectively Including Treats and Rewards

It's important to find a balance when using treats and rewards in dog training. For difficult assignments, give out high-value treats; for regular commands, give out lower-value treats. To avoid overindulging, break up treats into bite-sized pieces. Timing is crucial; to strengthen the bond, give a reward as soon as the desired behavior is demonstrated. Change up the rewards; include playtime, pats, and verbal praise in addition to treats. Reduce the frequency of treats gradually as your dog gains proficiency. This guarantees that they follow instructions genuinely understanding them and not just for rewards. When you use treats sparingly, you help your dog stay motivated during training by laying a solid foundation of trust and obedience.

CHAPTER THREE

Socialization and Behavior

Recognizing the Significance of Socialization

A dog that is well-rounded and well-adjusted needs to be socialized. It helps them become more adaptable and self-assured by exposing them to a variety of situations, people, animals, and surroundings. Early socialization ensures that they are at ease in a variety of settings and helps prevent fear and aggression. Positive interactions with other dogs are encouraged, which lessens the possibility of behavioral problems. Regular exposure to new stimuli aids in mental stimulation and prevents boredom. Additionally, a well-socialized dog is often more relaxed and enjoyable to be around, enhancing their overall quality of life. Prioritize socialization to raise a happy, confident, and socially adept canine companion who thrives in diverse environments.

Introducing Dogs to Different People, other Animals and Environment Introducing your dog to diverse environments, people, and animals is a crucial aspect of socialization. Begin in controlled, low-stress settings, gradually progressing to busier areas. Encourage pleasant encounters with various persons, ensuring they're comfortable around strangers. Expose children to diverse creatures, always prioritizing safety. This exposure promotes confidence and lessens fear or hostility towards strange creatures. Provide positive reinforcement for calm, friendly behavior. Through progressive, pleasant experiences, your dog learns to navigate new situations and encounters with confidence. This thorough socialization foundation cultivates a well-adjusted, confident

companion capable of thriving in a wide range of situations and places.

Managing and Correcting Unwanted Behaviors

Managing and correcting undesired habits is vital for a well-behaved dog. Begin by identifying the root cause of the behavior. Consistency is crucial; create clear standards and boundaries. Use positive reinforcement to encourage desired actions, while redirecting or ignoring unwanted ones. Employ moderate, effective corrections when appropriate, concentrating on redirection rather than punishment. Timing is essential; address the behavior quickly for the strongest impact. Be patient and persistent, as behavior improvement takes time.

CHAPTER FOUR

House Training and Crate Training

Establishing a designated Toilet Area

One of the most important parts of house training is setting up a separate bathroom area. Pick a location outside that your dog can get to with ease. Bring them here on a regular basis, particularly after meals and when they wake up. To help you associate it with the act, use a cue word such as "Go potty". Give them a treat and lots of praise when they relieve themselves in the designated area. Be patient since mistakes will be made while you are learning. If there is an accident inside, clean it up right once to get rid of any odor. Your dog will successfully complete house training if they are trained to associate the specified location with their bathroom needs through patience and continuous reinforcement.

Teaching your Dog to use a Crate

Your dog will have a safe and cozy place to live if you teach them to use a crate. Start by filling the crate with cozy toys and blankets. Treats within will promote exploration and good associations. Introduce brief periods of confinement gradually while praising composure. Never inflict punishment with the box.

Associate the container with pleasant occasions like meals and alone time. As your dog becomes used to its crate, gradually extend its stay. To make the crate feel like a secure refuge, be patient and give positive reinforcement. This ability offers a haven for your dog's wellbeing in addition to helping with housebreaking.

Establishing a Schedule for Meal Times and Rest Periods

A well-regulated dog needs a schedule for food times and toilet breaks. Maintaining consistency helps to avoid mishaps and gives structure. Set up regular feeding schedules, usually two or three times a day, to give them enough time to digest. Encourage them to use the potty outside right after meals and before going to bed. Make a timetable that fits their circadian rhythms and follow it religiously. Being predictable fosters trust and gives your dog a sense of security in their surroundings. This routine promotes their general health and well-being in addition to helping with house training.

CHAPTER FIVE

Walking Manners and Leash Training

Getting Your Dog Used to Wearing a Collar and Leash

A vital first step to safe and enjoyable walks with your dog is to ensure that they are comfortable wearing a collar and leash. Introduce the collar first in a serene, upbeat setting. Before you gently fasten, let them have a whiff and get acquainted with it. Choose a collar that fits well and is lightweight to guarantee comfort. Gradually come to associate wearing the collar, giving rewards, and receiving praise with happy events.

After that, bring the leash inside. To help your dog get used to the feeling, let them pull it around under supervision. Take up the leash gradually while rewarding good behavior. To gain confidence, go for quick, controlled walks inside.

When your dog is at ease wearing the collar and leash apart, put them together for quick walks outside in a calm, familiar setting. Treats and tender guidance will help them to grow. Keep the first

few meetings short and then progressively lengthen them as they get more comfortable.

It takes time for some dogs to adjust, so be patient. Refrain from yanking or pulling on the leash since this may be upsetting and unsettling. Instead, use positive reinforcement to nudge them to walk with you.

Positive associations and consistency enable your dog associate the leash and collar with good things, which opens the door to fun and safe walks together. Your dog will enthusiastically anticipate walks once it has had enough time and patience to learn to associate the leash and collar with good things.

Teaching Walking on a Loose Leash

A comfortable and regulated walking experience requires the teaching of loose leash walking. Start in a calm, comfortable setting. Make sure the collar or harness fits properly, and use a regular leash. Reward your dog for staying close and not pulling on the leash by starting with them on your left side.

Stop them when they start to tug and wait for them to come back to your side. A cue like as "walk" or "heel" can be used to indicate the intended action. When they comply, give them goodies, compliments, and a push in the right direction.

Reliability is essential. Practice often in different settings, adding distractions little by little. To keep their attention and excitement, keep training sessions brief and upbeat.

If your dog still pulls, you might want to use a head halter or no-pull harness to give them more control. Retractable leashes should be avoided as they promote tugging.

To recap, patience is essential. Dogs often need some time to get used to walking on a loose leash, particularly if they are pulleders. Remain steady and upbeat while lavishly thanking them for their hard work.

Managing Circumstances such as Pulling or Reacting to Distraction

An essential part of leash training is dealing with scenarios such as pulling or responding to distractions. Your dog should cease pulling and remain motionless. Refrain from pulling back since this could incite resistance. Prior to proceeding, wait for them to come back to your side. Utilize spoken cues such as "walk" or "heel" to reaffirm the intended behavior.

Redirect your dog's focus if they react negatively to distractions. To get them to focus again, give them toys, food, or a happy voice. Practice this in places that are regulated and have progressively more distractions.

Key is consistency. Use incentives and compliments to reinforce the desired behavior. Avoid becoming frustrated by being calm and patient. Recall that dogs require time to acclimate and learn.

For more control, especially if tugging continues, think about utilizing devices like head halters or no-pull harnesses. While you practice walking on a loose leash, these tools can offer further assistance.

It's critical to maintain initiative. Be ready to divert your dog's attention if necessary, and consider potential distractions beforehand. As their abilities grow, progressively expose them to more difficult settings.

Above all, give your dog nice walks. Encourage them with praise and give them chances to explore and smell. This promotes a favorable link between walking while wearing a leash.

CHAPTER SIX

Advanced Methods of Training

Agility and Trick Training

Dogs that participate in agility and trick training receive mental and physical stimulation, strengthening their bonds and improving their general wellbeing.

Speed and accuracy are required as you navigate an obstacle course during agility training. Strength, confidence, and coordination are all increased. Start with simple obstacles like tunnels and jumps and work your way up to more intricate courses. Give each successful attempt a reward by using positive reinforcement. Agility may be a fun competitive sport and helps to enhance physical fitness.

Trick training highlights the brains of your dog and adds a fun factor. Start with basic commands like "sit," "stay," and "paw," then work your way up to more complex ones like "roll over" or "play dead." Reward their achievements with praise and treats. In addition to stimulating your dog's intellect, trick training improves communication and fortifies your relationship.

For both agility and trick training, consistency, patience, and positive reward are essential. Sessions should be brief, interesting, and conclude positively. Make sure that the challenges and tricks you give your dog are challenging enough to keep them interested without becoming annoyed.

Above all, give your dog a good and fun training experience. It's a fantastic method to utilize their innate abilities and instincts, keeping them both physically and cognitively stimulated. It's also a lovely opportunity to bond with your pet and make treasured memories.

Targeting and Clicker Training

To teach dogs new actions and skills, clicker training and targeting are useful techniques that depend on positive reward.

The tool used in clicker training is a little, portable gadget with a distinctive clicking sound. When the dog does the required behavior, you click and the dog gets a treat or reward right away. Dogs can better grasp what behavior earned them a reward when they receive this clear, consistent signal. It is accurate and enables prompt reinforcement.

Teaching your dog to touch a particular object—typically with their nose or paw—is known as targeting. This could be your hand, a specified target stick, or a stick. You can train your dog to perform different poses or motions by teaching them to associate the touch with a command such as "touch" or "target." This technique enhances coordination, sharpens focus, and improves communication between you and your dog.

Patience, consistency, and repetition are necessary for both targeting and clicker training. These are adaptable methods that work with a variety of commands and gimmicks. As your dog gains experience, you can gradually stop using the target stick or clicker and just use verbal cues.

These techniques give your dog cerebral stimulation and make training sessions interesting. They create an environment that is conducive to learning, which produces a partner who is eager to learn and well-trained.

Dog Sport and Competitions

Dogs can be engaged and challenged through sports and competi tions, which can help to deepen the link between owner and pet. They provide a broad variety of exercises designed for various breeds and activity levels.

Popular sports like agility require players to navigate a course of obstacles like weave poles, tunnels, and jumps while racing against the time. It necessitates coordination, quickness, and accuracy.

Dogs compete in a fast-paced relay race called flyball, where they must jump hurdles to catch a ball and show off their speed and agility.

Dogs' capacity to obey directions in a regulated setting is evaluated through obedience trials, which also serve as a testament to their training and discipline.

Herding trials showcase a breed's innate ability for herding animals by having them steer and manage livestock along a predetermined path.

Dogs that perform dock diving jump from a dock into a pool to demonstrate their agility and retrieving prowess.

Disc dog contests highlight a dog's dexterity and agility through the catch and retrieval of flying discs.

For dogs and their owners, these sports provide socializing, mental and physical stimulation, and physical fitness. They also give dog lovers a place to interact and compete in a pleasant manner.

Dog athletes are challenged to perform to the best of their abilities and are encouraged to learn new things all the time. It's a fulfilling way to highlight your pet's skills and capabilities, giving you both a sense of pride and accomplishment.

CHAPTER SEVEN

Troubleshooting and Problem Solving

Recognizing and Handling Typical Behavioral Problems

It's critical to recognize and treat common behavioral problems in dogs in order to maintain a positive relationship and ensure their general wellbeing.

1. Aggression: Territoriality, fear, and social problems can all lead to aggression. It's critical to recognize triggers and seek professional advice for a customized behavior modification strategy.

2. Distress when left alone is a defining characteristic of separation anxiety. This problem can be lessened with gradual desensitization, the establishment of pleasant connections with departures, and mental stimulation.

3. Dogs that bark excessively may be doing so out of boredom, nervousness, or a craving for attention. Excessive barking can be curbed by treating the underlying reason and offering mental and physical activity.

4. Destructive Chewing: Boredom or worry are common causes of this practice. Engaging activities and the provision of suitable chew toys help redirect this behavior.

5. Dogs may jump up to attract attention or simply to get excited. This problem can be resolved by regularly reinforcing the "off" command and rewarding composed conduct.

6. Digging: This activity may be driven by impulse, boredom, or a need to desist. Creating a digging space, such as a sandbox, helps reroute this behavior.

7. Pulling on the leash: During walks, this is a regular problem. This can be addressed with the use of appropriate tools like a no-pull harness, consistent training, and positive reinforcement.

8. Medical conditions or inconsistent house training may be the cause of house soiling. This problem can be resolved by creating a routine, employing positive reinforcement, and, if necessary, seeing a veterinarian.

Identifying the underlying causes of these behavioral problems is essential to creating workable remedies. The keys to addressing and correcting these behaviors and producing a content and well-adjusted pet are persistence, patience, and positive reinforcement methods. It is advised to seek advice from a qualified dog trainer or behaviorist if issues continue.

Handling Fear, Anxiety, or Aggression

Dogs that exhibit aggression, anxiety, or fear need to be treated carefully and methodically in order to protect both themselves and people around them.

Hostility:

Recognize your triggers and stay out of hostile situations. For a behavior modification strategy that may include counter-conditioning, desensitization, and controlled exposure to triggers, speak with a specialist. Never discipline aggressive conduct since it may make the problem worse.

Unease:

Create a routine to offer stability and predictability. To establish positive associations with situations that cause anxiety, use positive reinforcement. Think about using products like anxiety wraps or relaxing pills. Anxiety levels can be lowered by gradual exposure to triggers, patience, and assurance.

Panic:

Respect their boundaries and refrain from using force. Building confidence requires both positive reinforcement and gradual exposure to frightening situations. By providing rewards and praise during these interactions, you can establish good associations. Seek expert assistance in times of extreme fear.

Being consistent is crucial while dealing with these problems. Steer clear of accidentally encouraging nervous or afraid behavior. Keep in mind that every dog is different, so it's important to customize your strategy to meet their particular needs. Seeking advice from a licensed behaviorist or veterinary behaviorist is advised in extreme circumstances.

Using positive reinforcement methods and establishing a calm, encouraging environment will help your dog overcome these obstacles and become a happier, more self-assured friend.

It is a reasonable and considerate choice to seek professional assistance for behavior problems with dogs or dog training. Veterinarian behaviorists and certified dog trainers have specific training and expertise that can be quite helpful when dealing with difficult or complicated issues.

Authorized Instructors

Professional dog trainers have undergone extensive instruction and evaluation, proving their competence in a range of training methods. They provide customized training schedules based on the

requirements of your dog. They can help with specific concerns like violence or anxiety as well as fundamental obedience and behavior management.

Behaviorists in Veterinarians

Veterinarians who have completed advanced training in animal behavior are known as veterinary behaviorists. They are qualified to identify and handle complicated behavioral disorders, frequently in addition to physical ailments. They are able to create intricate treatment plans and offer thorough examinations.

When to Get Expert Assistance

1. Severe Aggression: It's imperative to seek expert assistance if your dog exhibits aggressive behavior toward people or other animals, especially if it causes injury.

2. Severe Anxiety or Fear: In order to create a treatment plan that is effective, a professional may be necessary if your dog suffers from chronic anxiety or fear that significantly lowers their quality of life.

3. Persistent Behavioral Issues: A specialist can offer specific advice if your dog's behavior issues continue even after regular training sessions.

CHAPTER EIGHT

Maintenance and Continued Learning

Maintaining excellent behavior and a solid bond with your dog throughout their life depends on you continuing to reinforce training. Key is consistency. Refreshing their memory and reinforcing your directions can be achieved even after the initial training with periodic reinforcement sessions.

Frequent Practice: Daily routines might include brief, frequent training sessions. This improves the communication between you and your dog and keeps their abilities strong.

Changing Environments: To make sure your dog knows and obeys commands in a variety of settings, practice them in a variety of settings. This aids in extending their instruction outside of comfortable environments.

Create New Challenges: Keep adding new instructions or techniques. Dogs need mental stimulation to stay healthy and to avoid behavioral problems brought on by boredom.

Apply Positive Reinforcement: This effective strategy is still in use. Reward desired actions with fun, praise, and treats. This reaffirms their comprehension and encourages them to keep following the rules.

Correct Unwanted Behaviors: Take immediate action to address any new unwelcome behaviors. Redirect and reinforce the appropriate behavior by using positive reinforcement.

Remain Patient and Positive: Make sure that training sessions are fun and upbeat. Steer clear of irritation or frustration since these can impede growth. Regardless of how slowly things develop, there is always a happy ending.

Adapt to Age and Health: Modify training techniques to take your dog's age and health into account. Puppies need more time and patience, while older dogs could have different physical capacities.

Throughout your dog's life, you may retain a well-behaved, obedient companion by continuously reinforcing training. Additionally, it fortifies the link between you and your dog, fostering a happy and peaceful partnership for many years to come.

Including Enrichment and Mental Stimulation

A happy, well-mannered dog need mental stimulation and enrichment activities. Just as vital as physical exercise is mental exercise, which also helps avoid behavior problems stemming from boredom.

Puzzle feeders and toys: Interactive feeders and toys test your dog's ability to solve problems. They offer a gratifying method of dispensing meals or snacks in addition to stimulating the mind.

Training and Obedience: Keep teaching new instructions and maneuvers. This strengthens their training and arouses their cognitive capacities.

Scent Work: Play hide-and-seek or scent games to stimulate your dog's sense of smell. This stimulates their minds and appeals to their natural impulses.

Discover New Environments: Take your dog on walks or other excursions to other locations. The diversity of sounds, images, and smells enriches the mind.

Play Mind Games: Use puzzle games like "which hand" or "find the treat" to get kids thinking about solving problems. These are entertaining and thought-provoking games.

Rotate Toys and Activities: To keep things engaging and new, rotate toys and activities on a regular basis. By doing this, you may keep your dog from growing bored with its daily routine.

Use Food Puzzles: By making your dog struggle for their food, food puzzle toys stimulate their minds and satiate their innate desire to forage.

Offer Novel Experiences: To stimulate your dog's senses and maintain their curiosity, expose them to new things, such as various surfaces or textures.

You can maintain your dog's mental acuity and keep them happy and involved in their routine by providing mental stimulation and enrichment. This strengthens the link between you and your pet friend while also improving their general well-being.

Exploring Novel Training Tasks and Exercises

Introducing your dog to novel training exercises and challenges is a great approach to keep them mentally stimulated and learning new things all the time. It enhances their general well-being by offering mental and physical stimulation.

Advanced Obedience: Teach more intricate instructions or hone those that are already known to take basic obedience training to the next level. This strengthens your dog's training and tests his or her cognitive talents.

Specialized Training: Take into account courses in agility, search and rescue, or nose work. These games give your dog a fun and rewarding way to release their energy while also appealing to their natural inclinations.

Canine Sports: Take part in events such as fly ball races, obedience trials, and agility tournaments. These activities can be a wonderful way for you and your dog to interact while also offering the chance for friendly rivalry.

Therapy Work: If your dog is quiet and amiable, you could choose to train them for a therapeutic role. They can go to nursing homes, schools, or hospitals to offer consolation and company to people who are in need.

Herding Trials: You might think about taking part in herding trials if your breed is a herder. Your dog can demonstrate their innate herding abilities and instincts at these activities.

Involve your dog in the aquatic sport of dock diving, when they jump off a dock into a swimming pool. It's a fantastic method to get fun and workout together.

Learn to catch and retrieve flying discs for your dog to compete in disc dog competitions. A fun way to demonstrate their athleticism and coordination is to compete in disc dog tournaments.

Conclusion

To sum up, training your dog requires mutual understanding, patience, and persistence. It's a dedication to creating a solid and peaceful relationship with your animal friend. By devoting time and energy to training, you teach your dog the abilities they need to function in their environment.

The first stages are to recognize the significance of positive reinforcement, select appropriate training techniques, and create a regular routine. An appropriately socialized and obedient pet is the result of housebreaking, leash etiquette, and socialization.

With time, adding cerebral stimulation, trying out new things, and getting aid from a professional when necessary will make your dog's life better and extend their horizons. Keep in mind that every dog is different, so it's important to modify your technique to suit each dog's demands.

Rewarding relationships are created when instruction is reinforced throughout an individual's life, ensuring that they stay obedient and well-behaved. You provide them ways to exercise their bodies and minds, whether it's through agility, trick training, or dog sports.

Ultimately, training is about developing a strong bond based on mutual respect, trust, and communication rather than just giving orders. Your commitment to your dog's growth and well-being will surely result in a companion that is content, well-adjusted, and treasured for many years to come.

HAPPY DOG TRAINING.....